W9-CBC-393

Harriet Tubman

Marie Patterson, M.S. Ed.

Table of Contents

Dreaming of Freedom

Harriet Tubman was born a slave. But she dreamed of being free. In fact, she wanted all slaves to be free. As a young woman, Harriet escaped from slavery. She became a **conductor** (kuhn-DUCK-tuhr) on the **Underground Railroad**. She made 19 trips back to the South. Each time, she led slaves safely to the North. Harriet risked her own life and her freedom for others. She was a very brave woman.

▼ Map of Underground Railroad routes in Pennsylvania

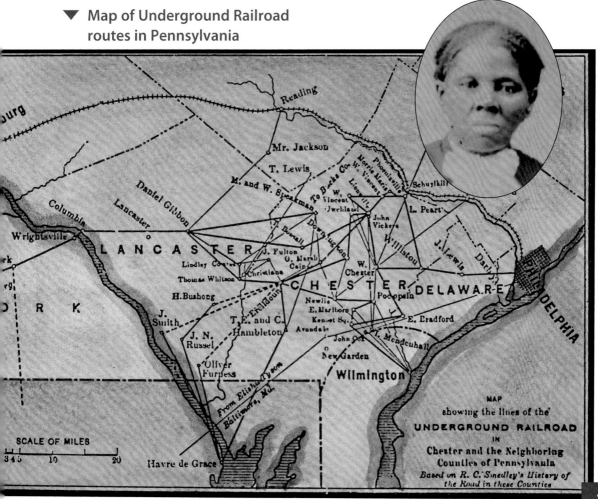

A Slave by Birth

When Harriet Tubman was born she was named Araminta (air-uh-MIN-tuh) Ross. Her nickname was Minty. She was born around the year 1820.

When she grew up, Minty went by the name of Harriet. This was also her mother's name. Her father was called Old Ben.

Harriet grew up on a **plantation** (plan-TAY-shuhn). Her home was on the Eastern Shore of Maryland. Harriet and her parents were slaves on the plantation.

▼ Slaves picking cotton on a plantation

▲ This is a typical slave cabin.

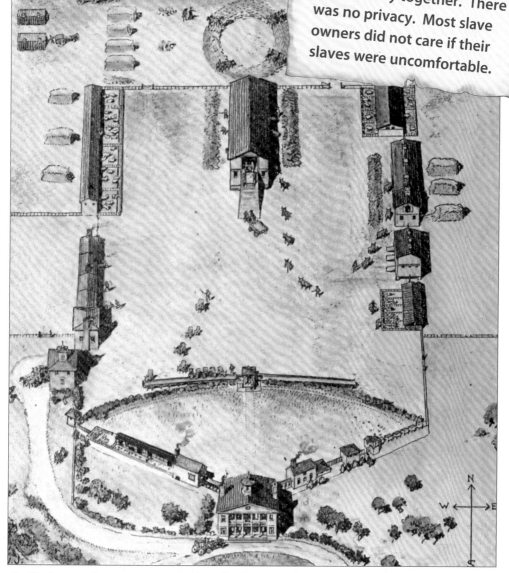

▲ Eighteenth-century Maryland plantation

Childhood on the Farm

Harriet was a slave because her parents were slaves. She had many brothers and sisters. Some of them worked for other farmers.

When Harriet was young, she played with the other children during the day. Her parents went to work in the fields. An elderly woman watched all the children while the parents worked.

◀ Slaves gathered in front of their small cabin

A slave picking ▶
cotton in the South

Burlap is a very rough fabric. ▶

A Tiny Wardrobe

Harriet did not have shoes, socks, shirts, or pants. The slave children received two burlap garments a year. If the clothes wore out, the children had to go without clothing until the next issue day.

▲ These cabins were built to show what slave cabins looked like.

At night, Harriet slept on the dirt floor of her family's cabin. Sometimes she listened to the adults talk about freedom. She did not know what freedom was. But it sounded wonderful. She wanted to learn more about it. When she was seven, Harriet tried to escape from the plantation. She did not succeed.

A Hard Life

At age five or six, most white children began school. But slave children were not allowed to go to school. Instead, at that age they began to work. At first, Harriet carried water to the workers in the fields. When she was six, her owner hired her out to work for the Cook family.

Harriet helped Mrs. Cook with weaving, cleaning, cooking, and serving. Mrs. Cook was mean to Harriet. She called her names like stupid and clumsy. Harriet also received many whippings. But, she still worked hard.

Another of Harriet's jobs was to watch Mr. Cook's **muskrat** traps. Muskrats were valuable as food and for their furs. When no one was looking, she loved to set the animals free and watch them swim away.

◀ Harriet wanted everything to be free, even muskrats.

Rec'd of Judge J Williams six hundred
Dollars in full payment for Lame a
negro woman 18 years old and henry her
Child about one year old together with her
future increase if any which negroes
I warrant to be sound in body and mind and
Slaves for life witness my hand and seal
this 20th Day of Decr 1849—

The conditions of the above instrument are
such that if the undersigned shall pay or cause
to be paid to Judge J Williams by the 1st Jan
1851 the sum of six hundred Dollars good and
lawful money the property as above described
to revert to the undersigned and the obligation
ment to be void, otherwise to remain in full
force and virtue this Day and [...]
[...] sealed and delivered in presence of
Test J. M. Lampley   John Wil[...]

[...] author Negroes sold [...]
sundry [...] Williams
and [...] money [...]

Slaves were often hired out to other plantation owners or sold. This is the sale document for one young woman.

Smart Thinking

Harriet was a clever girl. She learned to wear extra layers of clothing so she would not feel the beatings as much. She also learned to fake crying and pain. This made her master or mistress think she could not stand to be whipped anymore.

The Talk of Freedom

Harriet's owner continued to send her out to work for other people. She was frightened that she would be sent far away from her family. Farmers often sold difficult slaves to plantation owners in the deep South. The work was harder and the sun was hotter in these states. Some of Harriet's own brothers and sisters had been sold away. Somehow, though, Harriet stayed close to home.

This man is being sold away from his family.

A Tragic Incident

Harriet always stood up for others. As a young teenager she tried to stop an angry **overseer** from hitting another slave. Harriet was accidentally hit in the head with a heavy weight. She had headaches for the rest of her life.

Like Harriet, many ▶ other slaves wanted their freedom.

AM I NOT A MAN AND A BROTHER?

Harriet was curious when she heard the word *freedom*. When she was old enough to understand what it meant, she wanted it, too. Harriet tried to talk about freedom to her mother. But her mother was afraid to hear about it. However, Harriet's father was always willing to talk of freedom. Old Ben wanted to prepare his daughter to be free.

Mrs. Tubman

Harriet married John Tubman in 1844. John was a free man. This made Harriet want freedom even more. But John did not want Harriet to try to escape.

▲ Two newly married slaves get ready to jump the broom.

$150 REWARD.

RANAWAY from the subscriber, on the night of Monday the 11th July, a negro man named

TOM,

about 30 years of a___ dark col___ __r 7 inches high; of ___ several of his jaw ___ several old marks of ___own the back. He ___thing, and several ___ r his apprehension ___tate of Kentucky; ___ring on the Ohio ___rior counties ex- ___tter county.

L. BOSTON.

100 DOLLARS REWARD!

Ranaway from the subscriber on the 27th of July, my Black Woman, named

EMILY,

Seventeen years of age, well grown, black color, has a whining voice. She took with her one dark calico and one blue and white dress, a red corded gingham bonnet; a white striped shawl and slippers. I will pay the above reward if taken near the Ohio river on the Kentucky side, or **THREE HUNDRED DOLLARS,** if taken in the State of Ohio, and delivered to me near Lewisburg, Mason County, Ky.

THO'S. H. WILLIAMS.

August 4, 1853.

▲ Running away was very dangerous. These flyers describe slaves who had escaped.

Harriet's father disagreed with John. Old Ben taught Harriet about living in the woods. He believed that she needed to know how to **survive**. He also showed her how to follow the North Star. He taught her how to swim and start a fire. She learned how to catch and skin animals to eat.

Finally, Freedom

Harriet planned to run away several times. But, she always turned back because the time was not right. In 1849, she found out that she might be sold. This convinced her that it was time to escape.

This runaway ▶ is trying to avoid being returned to slavery.

▲ Slaves escaping on the Underground Railroad

Many people helped her along the way. It took days of running and hiding. Harriet finally made it to the free state of Pennsylvania.

Harriet found a job in Philadelphia, Pennsylvania. She worked hard and saved her money. Harriet wanted to help other slaves. She became the first female conductor on the Underground Railroad. It was a dangerous job, especially for an escaped slave.

Many runaway slaves felt safe when they made it to the free state of Pennsylvania. ▶

The Underground Railroad

The Underground Railroad was not under the ground at all. And, it was not really a railroad. It was a secret system planned by **abolitionists** (ab-uh-LISH-uhn-istz). They used it to help slaves escape to the North.

▼ These slaves are using darkness to hide their escape.

The slaves rested at "stations" or homes of people who disliked slavery. These people were stationmasters on the Underground Railroad. They told the slaves where the next safe station was.

The slaves watched for safe signs. The sign might be a whistle, a hanging quilt, or a candle in the window. If the slaves did not see the safe sign, they knew that slave catchers could be nearby.

▲ No one could tell that this house was an Underground Railroad station.

Fugitive Slave Act

Congress passed the Fugitive Slave Act in 1850. This law punished anyone who was caught helping runaway slaves. Some people became scared by this law. They would not help slaves escape anymore. But others were so angry about the law that they became even more determined to help.

Harriet to the Rescue

Harriet returned to slave **territory** (TAIR-uh-tor-ee) 19 times. She led many of her family members to freedom. In 1857, she rescued her parents. They were too old to walk. So, Harriet rented a wagon and drove them north.

Harriet also helped hundreds of others. She was never caught, and she never lost a slave along the way. Many times, she relied on her **instincts** (IN-stinkts) to get her to safety.

▼ Slaves escaping from the Eastern Shore of Maryland, like Harriet Tubman did

Harriet was very smart. She used many strategies to keep from being caught. She walked different routes. She brought along sleeping powder to quiet fussy babies. She wore disguises, even dressing as a man. Harriet carried a gun with her. She knew that the runaways might get scared and want to return to their farms. Harriet told them that they could not change their minds. They would be free or they would be dead.

Her Fame Grows

Harriet became famous. The Southerners were frustrated because they could not catch her. They offered a $40,000 reward for her capture. People compared her to the Biblical hero who led his people out of slavery in Egypt. They began to call Harriet, "Moses of Her People."

◀ This drawing shows Moses, the hero from the Bible.

▲ The Civil War began at Fort Sumter in Charleston, South Carolina.

The End of a Long Journey

After years of arguing, the people of the North and the South could not solve their problems. So, the southern states **seceded** (suh-SEED-ed) from the Union. This led to the United States Civil War. The first battle was fought in April 1861.

Harriet wanted to help the North during the war. She served as a nurse, scout, and spy for the Union army. Harriet had spent years traveling along the Underground Railroad. So, she knew the land very well. This was useful while she worked for the army.

One of her most important moments during the war happened in South Carolina. In June 1863, Colonel James Montgomery led a riverboat raid. Harriet served as his scout. During this raid, Harriet and Montgomery helped 750 slaves escape to freedom inside Union lines.

Harriet Tubman served as a ▶ scout for the Union Army.

John Brown

John Brown's Raid

An abolitionist named John Brown believed slavery was a sin. He gathered a group of 21 black and white men. This group tried to steal some guns to give to slaves. Harriet supported John Brown and even considered joining him on this raid. It is a good thing she did not because many of the men were killed. Brown was arrested. Later, he was hanged for what he did.

William Lloyd Garrison

Frederick Douglass

Well-known Abolitionists

Harriet Tubman was an abolitionist who fought to end slavery. There were other well-known abolitionists during the years before the war. Frederick Douglass was a slave in Maryland. In 1838, he escaped to New York.

William Lloyd Garrison was a well-known white abolitionist. One day Garrison heard Douglass speak. Garrison asked Douglass to travel with him and tell people about his life as a slave. Douglass became a famous speaker. He was very **passionate** (PASH-uh-nut) about freeing the slaves.

Slave Narratives

It was very important for slaves to tell others about their experiences. One way that they did this was through slave narratives. These were oral or written descriptions of what it was like to be a slave. Frederick Douglass wrote his story in the book, *The Narrative of the Life of Frederick Douglass*. This book describes life as a slave on the Eastern Shore of Maryland. Then, it tells how Douglass escaped and what he did to help end slavery.

Harriet Tubman believed in the cause of freedom. Her efforts continued after slavery ended in the United States. She built a home in New York for elderly blacks who had no place to live. She also told women to "stand together" when they fought for the right to vote. Harriet died at the age of 93. She was one of the bravest "soldiers" of her time.

▼ This is 91-year-old Harriet Tubman in New York.

Glossary

abolitionists—people who were against slavery and worked to end it

burlap—a heavy, woven material that feels rough

conductor—a guide; someone who helped escaped slaves get to the North

customs—things that are passed down from generation to generation; traditions

instincts—natural feelings about something

master—the male who is the head or boss of the slaves; usually the owner of the plantation

mistress—the female who is the head or boss of the household slaves; usually the plantation owner's wife

muskrat—a water rodent that has glossy brown fur and webbed feet

overseer—someone who worked on a plantation; this person's main job was to discipline and control the slaves

passionate—feeling something very strongly

plantation—a large farm in the South that produced crops for money

seceded—pulled out or withdrew from something; states that left the Union

survive—to stay alive

territory—an area of land outside a country's borders

Underground Railroad—the secret system for slaves to escape to the North